*Torching the Brown River*

*Torching the Brown River*
LORNA SHAUGHNESSY

**salmon**poetry

Published in 2008 by
Salmon Poetry,
Cliffs of Moher, County Clare, Ireland
Website: www.salmonpoetry.com
Email: info@salmonpoetry.com

Copyright © Lorna Shaughnessy, 2008

ISBN 978-1-903392-77-5

All rights reserved. No part of this publication may be reproduced or transmitted in any form or by any means, electronic or mechanical, including photography, recording, or any information storage or retrieval system, without permission in writing from the publisher. The book is sold subject to the condition that it shall not, by way of trade or otherwise, be lent, resold or otherwise circulated without the publisher's prior consent in any form of binding or cover other than that in which it is published and without a similar condition, including this condition, being imposed on the subsequent purchaser.

Cover artwork: Fintan Convery
Cover design & typesetting: Siobhán Hutson

For Fintan, Barra and Mark

## *Acknowledgments*

Acknowledgements are due to the editors of the following publications in which a number of these poems first appeared:

*Crannóg, Cyphers, The Burning Bush, The SHOp, The Stinging Fly, The Sunday Tribune, West47.*

To the editors of Arlen House and Windows Publications for poems included in their respective anthologies *Divas* and *Authors and Artists*.

And to Lapwing Press for those poems collected in the 2005 pamphlet *Song of the Forgotten Shulamite*.

## Contents

| | |
|---|---|
| Sea Change | 13 |
| The Charm | 14 |
| Song of the forgotten Shulamite | 15 |
| Signing | 16 |
| Dawn Arrival | 17 |
| Causeways | 18 |
| Cross-beams | 19 |
| Coming out of Stars | 21 |
| Disarray | 22 |
| Ambush | 23 |
| The photographs they never took of the life they almost shared... | 24 |
| Making Tracks | 25 |
| Eurydice to Orpheus | 26 |
| Unsung | 27 |
| The Funeral | 28 |
| Lost for Words | 29 |
| Guadalupe, Tonantzín | 30 |
| Guadalupe | 31 |
| Drawing from the Well | 32 |
| Imbolc | 33 |
| Grasping the Nettle | 35 |
| Achilles' Heel | 36 |
| Threads | 38 |
| Newgrange, New Millennium | 39 |

| | |
|---|---|
| Primum Mobile | 40 |
| Detail from "The Aldobrandini Madonna" | 41 |
| Gorse Fire | 42 |
| Antigone | 43 |
| Euripides writes to his pupil from exile in Macedonia... | 44 |
| Dreamless Streets | 45 |
| Our Lady of the Lilacs | 46 |
| Bush Drums | 47 |
| The Careless Genie | 48 |
| Song of Expectancy | 49 |
| Naranjo en flor | 50 |
| Empty Pockets | 51 |
| Epiphany | 52 |
| Appointment with Mutilation | 53 |
|   *Via Cruxis* | |
|   *Post op* | |
|   *Convalescence* | |
|   *The Flesh* | |
| Taliswomen | 56 |
| True Aim | 57 |
| Drinking Lemonade with Whistler's Mother | 58 |
| Impressionist | 59 |
| Heart-stopper | 60 |

## Sea Change

*For Trish*

The day the tide turned at her feet
she discovered her true nature;
a mirror flashed, a silver tail flipped
and she swam into her element.

Now waves swell in her blue-green eyes,
her ear strains to catch her sisters' song,
and salt dries in the hollow prints
where she walks.

Pearls scatter in her hair, to crown
the changeling, and call to mind
an older charm, the caul, a sign
this child would never drown.

## *The Charm*

Love had made them wild and timid
as hares driven to the wilderness,
the unsought rocky headlands
only stumbled on by the rest,
their bodies uncharted
as the stony shorelines where they ran.

Alert to the intruder's step,
swift in retreat to the walls of intimacy,
austere and rich as solitude,
unprepared to meet the eye that would break the spell
and make them shed their tawny coats,
lose their keenness of ear,
to be again a thing of goose-pimpled flesh
walking upright, visible and bare.

## Song of the forgotten Shulamite

Who will sing for the ageing Shulamite,
who will share her song?
See how her limbs bow like branches
burdened with unplucked fruit,
her skin dulls like dust-coated foliage.


Who will dance with the ageing Shulamite,
who will clasp her waist and move
her creaking branches in the wind?
Hear how her feet drag across the floor
as the rustling of dry leaves.


Who will love the ageing Shulamite,
who will be her King?
Lift up her boughs, lift up her head
and crown her hair with flowers,
that she may once again stand tall
among the Cedars of Lebanon.

# *Signing*

*For Joanna and her son Gabriel*


You speak my language.
The dart and lunge of your hands startle,
twin kingfishers on this brown river.

The Glen encircles us
like the nest we found under the apple tree,
a weave of horsehair and moss
braided through with memories.

You speak your father's tongue as well.
No more owned by place than the migrant in flight,
effortless, heart-rending and spell-breakingly
you glide between your parents' worlds,
between speech and silence –

the air that hums between feathers on the shaft of a wing,
the hushed anticipation of nestling eggs.

## *Dawn Arrival*

Lemon-rind moon. The road is mine,
but the town belongs to the crows
that swoop low across the litter-filled square,
earlier still than the Brazilians
who huddle in the wing mirror against the chill,
heads turning at the rumble of diesel engines
accelerating past them and on to the open road.

Faded letters fall from my name
on a shop-front in this, the seat of my tribe.
The dawn, tentative, picks its way west
lit by hawthorn, reluctant clouds blush
then dissolve into blue.

A jet-stream carves a skewed horizon
that splits sky from sky and for a moment
seems to set limits on boundless space.
Your plane descends as though drawn
by an invisible line back to earth,
the pull of the migrant's flight-path.

## *Causeways*

Snow on Popocatépetl, the Sleeping Woman[*]
yawns and stretches, a half-moon smiles
crookedly as the last lights go out in the valley
and the parched city licks the hillsides.

A blurred photograph falls from a wallet,
lovers seated on basalt columns an ocean away,
her arms bind his chest in a tight girdle
as though her life depended on it,
as though he could stop the wind
that whips their clothes and hair.

In eighty-five the gods thrashed in their graves,
the city shook, schools and hospitals crumbled;
only the infants in their incubators were spared.

Elsewhere their anger oozed and oozes still,
the slow-cooling fire that sculpted enigmatic causeways,
hexagonal puzzles where giants and lovers
pitch their wits against the elements.

---

[*] Popular name for Iztaccíhuatl, a dormant volcano. Both Iztaccíhuatl and the highly active Popocatépetl are situated in the Central Mexican altiplano.

## *Cross-beams*

A full moon casts sheet ice on the Moyle.
Even on a windless night like this
things disappear,
mottled clouds that interrupt the moonlight,
the lights of fishing boats huddled
like a village on a wide valley floor,
the throb of their engines
gone by the time we make the next curve in the road.

Birdwing whirrs in the gorse
that smelled of coconut this afternoon,
odourless now in the moist stillness.
Our steps startle a ewe and her lamb
as we shrink back to the warmth of the car
and switching off the headlamps, climb from Dan Nancy's
to meet the beam from Rathlin's southern shore,
a path on the black water of solid light.

At Torr Head we scramble
round the coastguard's ruined watch.
You tell me how they torched it
in the 'twenties, and how a poet
almost came to live here, to watch,
perhaps, for beams of lighthouses
we cannot quite make out.

On our way back down, a rising sea-mist
fingers the barbed wire fences.
Cushendun is clear,
lights reflect in the harbour,
a buoy winks, a solitary car
makes its way along the Layd road
and beyond, the odd faint light in Glenarriff.

Even on a windless night like this
things disappear.
Mars burns to our South
and overhead, where the plough should be,
a question mark hangs in the sky.

## Coming out of Stars

Once I saw the heavens migrate,
take the forms of creatures,
not lions, rams or scorpions
but gold and turquoise fish
that swam in the fathomless heights.

I had forgotten the many colours of the stars.

Last night they took flight
swift and sudden as starlings
but silent, silent as silver.
They rose in a bright arc, a surging wave,
swooped earthwards
and opened like a fan
to form trunk, limb and branch,
a tree of star starlings
that beckoned with its throbbing light.

Rapt as a nocturnal flower
that has long forgotten the sun
I close my eyes and see it still,
still long to be swept up
to sing like a bird on any of its branches.

## *Disarray*

The gales have passed
but bits of her are scattered
from Spiddal to the Coral Strand.
She hastens to gather them up,
blocked by Sunday drivers
with tidier lives, and sees
the pieces do not make a pretty picture,
some are missing, or else
there are just too many.

The heat in this November sun is unseasonal;
the heart the only true barometer.
She saw it coming that afternoon in August
when she switched on her wipers
to clear the dandelion snow.

## *Ambush*

Brutality was not
what sprang to mind in the afterglow.
Neither of them saw it coming
as they dressed hurriedly and walked,
without touching, to the car.
But it stopped him in his tracks
when the words *this is pointless*
sprang from the shadows.

Next day when he asked
she could not recall the words on her lips,
but felt the rawness of the wound
they had opened, point-blank.

## *The photographs they never took of the life they almost shared...*

would include a young woman, a bag slung over her shoulder smiling from the steps of a museum. Their legs just touching beneath a café table over breakfast. That moment of realisation in a young man's eyes, the same look in an older man's eyes as she walked across a crowded bar in a city she had left behind. A drive into western light, her hand on the nape of his neck, or the lakes and mountains she saw in his eyes when they made love between the cool sheets of a morning mist. The suddenness of two hares oblivious to the clicking shutters of memory as the present wraps itself in the safe blanket of the past, a life of snapshots to catalogue, paste in albums that gather dust in dark corners.

## *Making Tracks*

A heron takes off from a perch of rusted scrap
as the train pulls away;
she kissed him on the cheek as she left,
wanting things to be right.

The girl on the other side of the table
turns a new leaf of her paperback,
*Shaken, not Stirred*
as they rattle along worn tracks.

Sunlight glances off the backs of gulls, insolent.
The train shudders past the wastelands
that follow every track leaving town
till it decides which direction to take.

She tucks her punched ticket into a back pocket,
jolted by contrapuntal rhythms
and looks for her fate
in the name of every station.

## Eurydice to Orpheus

What was it you doubted, Orpheus,
as you emerged towards the light?
Was it the sureness of my step
or the grace of your gift?

Oh poet of great power and little faith
who charmed the creatures with your song
and still could not believe the given thing.

Did you even hear my echoing foot-fall
on the road out of hell,
or were your ears filled
with the pulsing fear of your own blood?

Easier to blame my constant and unfaltering feet,
turn loss to contempt
and scorn my Thracian sisters.

Some say your head rolled to Lesbos.
I doubt it.
The sweet chords of your faithless gift
will long outlive this song.

## *Unsung*

Is it so hard to write, that song about the men
who came from grey towns that smelled of turf smoke,
where crows painted invisible arcs
in low clouds around high nests,
a tragic chorus accompanied mostly by dogs?
Where women folded their cardiganed arms
and talked bittertalk in the black rectangles
of doors that opened to dark, narrow houses?

Men who left to find something better,
found it, then found they had to leave again;
who girded up their resolve and clenched their jaws
as they took the boat, cut adrift
from the smiles and wet kisses of babes,
and who knows if the words they wrote home,
like the strong hand that rubs a bruised shin,
ever took the edge off the pain?

Robbed of their children's childhood,
the good fathers who look, surprised,
at middle-aged sons and daughters,
still hoping to catch a glimpse of those little faces.

# The Funeral

*For Gerard Falvey*

"Plastic Paddy" he called himself,
and was genuinely surprised
when his dead uncle showed up in a dream
in the driver's seat, taking him
to an unnamed destination.

It was the call of the tribe.

Taking his father's place at the funeral,
in the front line now, shoulder to shoulder
with men who forgave imperfection
in death as in life, wishing only
for this in their final hour:

to bring home their own,
carry them back to summer mischief,
the licence of kinship, and here, now,
the familiarity of a hand on the shoulder
of his best coat, a whisky pressed into his hand.

## *Lost for Words*

Here was a man with plenty to say
but somehow no language ever said enough.
He picked them up like cheap souvenirs
of other people's lives in exotic places
observed through a lens of professional disinterest,
and professed a preference not to speak
the language of his youth
but rather held it at arms' length,
some kind of primitive specimen,
the mother tongue that licks the wound.

## Guadalupe, Tonantzín *

*For Estelle*

If black is the absence of colour
the night sky is not black
but has many hues.
Like pain,
a raven's wing,
Tonantzín's hair.
And the souls of those
untouched by this world
shine in the blue of her mantle
like stars in a lightening sky,
brushing the dark skin
of her mother's arms
that open in embrace
in the blackest of nights.

\* According to a 17th century legend, the Virgin of Guadalupe appeared to the Indian peasant Juan Diego on a mountainside long associated with worship of the Aztec Goddess Tonantzín. Guadalupe is traditionally depicted as dark-skinned, and wears a blue, star-studded mantle.

## *Guadalupe*

We climb the steps
and pin a little miracle to the altar –
a shrunken heart of brass.
Old women open and close their fish mouths,
hands weaving spells around each others' heads
and fasten gaudy ribbons
at the saint's feet.

We walk along one hundred years
of thankful witness, hand-painted
by souls who saw and survived:
revolution, fire, a train-crash, open heart-surgery,
lives walked in pilgrimage down long avenues
named in victorious optimism
to Guadalupe's ochre domes.

In the museum, a bird builds her nest
among coyotes and flowers, another perches
on the patriot-priest's shoulder and sings
about the day a brown saint met a brown goddess,
her feet in the river, the stars in her mantle
as watchful as the eyes of the dead.

On the trinket-seller's stall,
wrapped in the national flag,
Guadalupe smiles down
on dark-skinned cherubs
wearing Indian clothes.

## *Drawing from the Well*

In a pub that fills on Brigit's day
a lone whistle gives a last gasp
and a drunk singer stands berated.
We lift the latch, and his song veers off its stave
as we enter a room of shifting looks and feet
and take our place at the table by the fire.

My friend draws back the bow
of the dead man's fiddle
hung silent on the wall ten years
and follows the whistle's lead.
The woman of the house
conducts her unruly clients,
and memories of a brother's music
work a saint's charm on arthritic fingers.

Like Brigit's cloak the tunes unfurl,
seamless, unchecked, spilling from bar to street
round and round the statue to hover over offerings
– a bowl of white hyacinths, beads, a Matchbox car –
fanning the candles' crazed dance in the draught of the well
then skimming over water, upstream,
to wind around the cross.

Dust, raised by each stroke of the fiddler's bow
sparkles in the sun that warms her shoulder;
our eyes fix on the compelling pendulum
of motes as they settle in slow motion on her hair.
She nods and winds the music down,
drawing the cloak back in
to hang it on a sunbeam,
then hands the fiddle back across the bar.

01.02.03

## *Imbolc*

*For Mary, Sue and the Kiloughery brothers*

More frozen than chosen people
we add our voices to the prayers,
bear witness to the weaving of a cross,
each rush an outward-reaching spoke
in the seasons' turning wheel,
observe the sure-handed women
who anoint the heads of souls
– straight or stooped –
those left behind and those
who chose blessed solitude.

More tentative than sure
I place an offering at the well,
my breath suddenly caught
by the sense that all these supplications
even whispered here and now
would drown the music of running water.

Clutching our hot whiskies
we huddle by the fire. Again,
Sue plays Paddy Kiloughery's fiddle
and Locksey would have us stay
for the session and *The Whores of Soho,*
and stay we would
were it not for the wains
and the yoga classes…

The cold air outside the pub breaks the charm;
we aim for Black Head in the last light.
A mile away, cranes loom above the cliffs,

traffic management, portacabins,
an empty carpark on the wrong side of the road
soon to be filled with coaches
when the summer ritual begins.

Our laughter at the signs of progress has an edge.
The car swallows space and harnesses time,
I glance in the rear-view mirror
sensing Brigit at our backs,
around us still, the caim.

01.02.05

## *Grasping the Nettle*

Nothing stings the memory like nettles.
I squeeze the sap from a dock leaf onto a small hand
and recall a girl who tried to jump a stream, stumbled,
clutching wildly at the first solid-looking clump of green,
not pausing to measure stream, leg or consequence
and the shocked revelation of pain
that screamed from hand to brain.

She entered the street stage right, hand held aloft
like a messenger from the battlefield.
Her uncle shook his head and held the hand
beneath a tap outside the byre.

And it was hard to tell which gave the sharper sting,
the blisters rising on her palm, the icy shock of water,
or the salty taste of shame on her lips.

## *Achilles' Heel*

Jaws drop around the table
as the story unfolds
of how the fearless Achilles
met his destiny at Troy.

Agamemnon the school-yard bully
angling for a fight, Helen's flight
only there to drive the plot, raise anchors
and hoist a thousand sails to the wind.

Behind the epic glamour and gore
young minds ponder
profound injustice,
the tragic flaw.

What was she thinking
when she dipped her child so carelessly?
Couldn't she have held one foot first
and then the other, have the river
cover him all over?

Implacable logic. Blame
must be apportioned where it's due.
Achilles, arrogant and feared,
in these young minds the victim
of a mother's oversight.
God knows they see it every day.

And any mother worth her salt
would take more care
when following divine instruction.
Instead the hero's one true weakness
won him his fame; the softest tissue,
fatally exposed, brought him
to the river's farthest shore.

# *Threads*

The neighbours must think she's cracked:
my mother, a sensible woman
not given to eccentricities, smiles
and hangs doll's clothing on the line.
Fabrics unseen in twenty-five summers
as vivid now as the flowers she planted in spring.

Paisley was all the rage then, and crocheted capes;
my sisters stitched and hooked sixties haute couture
for the best-dressed dolls in Candahar Street,
each stitch the work of small hands and big ideas.

She gathers in her multi-coloured harvest,
the steam-iron hisses, strokes away each crease,
fondly teases each pleat and tuck into its rightful place.
Sisters gasp at their own artfulness as names
come flooding back – Tressie, Sindy, Joyce – I finger
the tiny garments and wonder at the scale of their perfection.

My belly swells more with each season. Early spring
and friends bring fairy clothes for the coming child.
I hang them on the line, and note
a stitch is called for here and there.

## *Newgrange, New Millennium*

*For I am every dead thing
In whom love wrought new alchemy.*

    John Donne

TV lights glare in the eye of a solstice dawn,
the man with the microphone
mouths tired words. Silent

as the womb the chamber waits,
greets the first light
with the mute solemnity of stone.

Hand on belly, I turn inwards
to miracles unseen,
waiting for the moment of recognition.

## *Primum Mobile*

Not even Michaelangelo
could capture the power
in this tiny hand
that spans my heart,
holds me in its palm.

## *Detail from "The Aldobrandini Madonna"*

*O that you would kiss me with the kisses of your mouth!*
    (Song of Songs 1.2). Epigraph on seventeenth century
    print of Titian's "Aldobrandini Madonna"

*And when Elizabeth heard the greeting of Mary,*
*the babe leaped in her womb* (Luke 1.41)

Something leaps within me.
Older than Elizabeth and not barren,
my eyes are stung
by this sudden intimacy.

The infant's arm stretches up
as though to take the measure of anticipation.
Saint Catherine's mouth draws closer,
so close now he can feel the heat of her breath.

Mary's blue sleeve draws them in,
an arching sky about their heads,
waves of silk lap at Catherine's knees.
Together they are an island.

Drenched I wade to its shore.

## Gorse Fire

The day before the resurrection
we gathered egg-shaped pebbles on the beach,
fingering their punished perfection,
now the painted eggs we hid in the garden
are lost – or too well hidden.

The stone is rolled back
but the women find only the burial clothes.
Someone forgot to tell the bees
and they will not return to the hive.

The gorse banks up the hillside like a Cathedral choir
sending up its shouts of joy. The Glen ignites
as the evening sun sparks off the yellow flowers,
torching the brown river
with the promise of Pentecostal fire.

# *Antigone*

> *You have dishonoured a*
> *living soul with exile in the tomb.*
>     Sophocles

*In memoriam Jean McConville*

The last time I saw you, daughter,
you were coming back from the shop;
you didn't even drop the messages
and only broke into a run
after they bundled me into the car,
the shopping clutched to your breast.

Rumour seeps onto the streets
like poisonous gas, corrupting the dead.
My memory, buried alive,
scrapes at earth and stones
with nails that keep growing.

Alive and still unheeded,
your requests always untimely
in the ears of important men. Too young
you learned about the silence of the grave,
looking down for signs.

And my bones lit up the dark soil
like a portentous constellation
neither I nor my children can read.

Antigone, speak to us now,
raise your voice above
the trite moralities of the chorus.
We know the price we have paid,
can you tell us what it is
we have bought?

## *Euripides writes to his pupil from exile in Macedonia...*

Rain-sodden sparrows peck
the last spilt seeds from my doorstep,
my bones ache from the damp.
I wish I could summon
in my heart such courage
as I penned in the young girl's mouth, who,
knowing the winds would not change
for any miracle or sacrificial blood,
that men would set a thousand sails
against their better senses,
laid bare her neck to the knife
and shamed the House of Atreus.

This war has lodged itself
in my memory and in my lungs
and nothing I write seems to dock
in the safe harbour of conclusion.

Take this sad tale where you will,
raise its anchor from my heart
and cast it adrift.  Clouds
darken the horizon.

## *Dreamless Streets*

> *Oh little town of Bethlehem*
> *how still we see thee lie.*
> *Above thy deep and dreamless sleep*
> *The silent stars go by.*

Bone-weary
we cross dusty plains,
the nights unnaturally lit
brighter than moonlight.

Drunk soldiers stagger at the city gates,
we make ourselves small to pass
and find Bethlehem a garrison town
that reeks of liquor and fear.

Dark figures shrink into doorways
as church bells sound the curfew.
A stray dog barks. We pick our way
through broken glass.

How often must we return to the place of birth?
A baby cries, voices rise in anger,
I hear the donkey's feet on the cobbles
and watch our shadows
lengthen in the starlight.

## *Our Lady of the Lilacs*

In the month of Our Lady, I brought
Protestant lilacs to school for the May altar.
My favourite lady lived next door, where
small, sceptered rituals set me apart,
a stool of my own by the hearth,
milk from a china cup.

Later, I sent postcards
from Zanzibar and Chichicastenango
to grace her mantelpiece, confident
my wanderlust would raise a smile,
recalling shared territories of the past,
the thrill of sunsets and palm trees
slotted through the letterbox,
postcards my father sent from hot,
far-fetched places.

I loved the smell of her powder,
the delicacy of her cheek and her unfading
Church of Ireland choir-singer's voice.
Christmas after Christmas, three perfectly parcelled
flasks of talc for Jim and Kathleen's girls and then,
the widower's voice on the line –

"Gladys is passed away".

Gladys Heath of number thirty-two Candahar Street,
your church-going decency such a part of this place
and yet so rare. In these mis-spelt imperial reaches,
across the Lagan from the Holy Land,
the waters of the river never did part
nor Moses lead us to safer shores.

## *Bush Drums*

The bins are silent.

That shuddering, shock-inducing clatter of lids
that sent cats into scalded vertical flight,
the tribal warning system of danger and predation
replaced by the weekly grumble
of plastic wheels on tarmac.

Some would have it the past is a foreign country,
that certain cultural practices are best put aside,
that wheelie-bins are one of the lesser dividends
of peace in our time.

## *The Careless Genie*

There is a kind of magic
that never learned the art of good timing,
the genie who pops up too late
and finds a child sick with wishing
who looks dully at the jeweled turban,
shrugs, and asks if he too
can live in a bottle?

## Song of Expectancy

(After George Hitchcock)

I wait for the train that never comes.
I wait for those who were not lost
I wait to see their faces on the platform,
shell-shocked, bleached by lack of sleep,
I wait to lead them out of tunnels
I wait for the bitter olives to ripen
I wait for storks to nest on my rooftop
I wait for signs, for the right constellation
of tea-leaves in my cup, the last shot
that ricochets round the square,
I wait for the rain to wash the dust
from the leaves of the orange trees,
I wait beside last year's timetable
on a peeling wall
with my spilt cup
for the train that never comes
my face bone white
with the pain of hope.

## *Naranjo en flor*

I remember perfectly
the awkward gait of storks
bending branches
as they landed in the olive trees,
still hear the fountains
in gardens haunted by sad princes,
sense the presence of small squares
in the dark, where orange trees flower
and petals form crystals on cobblestones.

But I cannot smell the orange-blossom
or feel the touch of your hand.

## *Empty Pockets*

There was a time
when I stuffed my pockets
full of summer,
shells, smooth stones,
a gull's feather.

There was a time
when my feet answered
your unerring rhythm,
scrunching over stones,
our talk fading with the light
as pebbles chimed, dragged
by the ebbing tide
out into the dark.

There was a time
when things held meaning,
hieroglyphs of a shared memory –
stone, shell, feather.

## *Epiphany*

Fairy lights cast shadows upwards
through the Christmas tree
making patterns on the ceiling,
dark snowflakes in a white sky.

Time to put away the tinsel.

Soon the branches will kindle,
each twig sparking before it blooms
and bows with a dying fall,
the wounded choreography
that still quickens the blood
in the cooling from blaze to ash.

Outside, a pine tree creaks in the wind
like the hinges of a closing door.

# *Appointment with Mutilation*

*Via Cruxis*

Is this how the young Masai feel
as they walk the tunnel that opens onto pain,
greet the knife that cleaves
past life from future?

Five minutes from ward to surgery
could be an eternity. Somehow
feet find a way of moving forward.
Bolting is no longer an option.

The lift descends. One floor down
a porter wheels in an empty chair,
in courtesy looks away from my wet face.
Doors part onto polished tiles,
the sudden agoraphobia of the last stretch.

A paper hanky is offered,
one hand beneath my elbow guides,
another presses my shoulder;
compassion ushers in surrender.

*Post op*

Focus, focus on the words, eyes, touch,
breath in the oxygen from the mask.
The only pain I feel is in my arm.

Back on the ward,
a woman from Casla and her daughter-in-law
tear strips off uncompliant kin.
I vomit on the other side of the curtain.

For a split second your eyes register disbelief,
the words slip out "That's bile, love",
you stroke my hair and wet my lips.

I ride waves of biliousness,
a sea of senseless motion,
the only unmoving point your hand.


*Convalescence*

Propped on pillows
too tired for tears
I hear sound-bites of the paper
I asked you to read.
At midday we switch on the telly
for TG4s re-runs of The Virginian,
double bill. All these years
and Trampas hasn't changed a bit.

Then things get fuzzy,
the reception is bad
or else the morphine is good.

Slowly, the ear attunes
to the language of nerve-endings:
*paravertebral block, PCA, Difene,*
and conjugations of caring too subtle to index
in the grammars of behaviour in good health.

I learn to accept the routine delicacy
of extraordinary kindness.

*The Flesh*

Wing-clipped.
This rite of passage has cut a path
from shoulder blade to rib-cage,
moved muscle, removed
that part of me lately defined undesirable,
undesired.

The scars will fade.
Inside, living tissue twists and stretches,
finds ways to accommodate a new anatomy
as the hawthorn bows to Atlantic gales,
wind-warped,
forsaking symmetry for survival.

# Taliswomen

*For Pura*

The handful of dolls you gave me
come to the day-ward in my pocket.
Each face embroidered with her own humour,
each *huipil*, woven in Chiapas, tells a story,
each woman bald beneath her bright headscarf,
the tell-tale sign that marks us all.

The poisoned chalice is hooked up
by the gloved hands of administering angels.
Even clad in latex their touch transcends
the banalities that spew from daytime radio;
some one thing
       inviolable.

## *True Aim*

Despite her stature
she always saw herself as an Amazon
but baulked at the price of amputation
just to draw back the bowstring faster.

Now the deed was done
would she feel the tension of string against her cheek,
release the arrow from its wounded nest,
observe its flight and fall
far from her quiver full of fears?

## *Drinking Lemonade with Whistler's Mother*

No, this is not how I remembered you:
your mouth never made a straight line,
your mirth fizzed those afternoons
drinking lemonade on the veranda,
recounting childhood escapades,
or gazing toward the lake
across well-trodden grass,
respectful of all that went before,
attuned to the voices calling from the garden
you touched my hand and smiled
"Go now, they're waiting".

## *Impressionist*

Your voice chimes amidst the china,
the soft thock of croquet on the lawn.
A painter's brush traced that shadow
on your brow, the drape of your skirt, just so.
"Come and laugh with us" you say,
but I cannot hear my voice.

Your hand strokes the varnished wood
that sweeps upwards to white rooms
where I am clothed in muslin and lace,
satin slippers placed on my feet,
a gardenia at my breast.
"Look in the mirror" you say,
but I cannot see my face.

"Link arms with me" you say,
"and let us stroll by the lakeshore".
The curve of our bustled backs mirrored by swans
who turn their heads in recognition as we glide by.
Poised in perfect stillness
the water shows me the possibility of grace,
but still, I cannot see my face.

## *Heart-stopper*

Many trees grow in the walled garden of my heart,
clipped and teased to a topiary of delight.
Shy camels graze on tender shoots
that sprout between old stones,
blinking in the stillness.

But not for long.

Enter cymbals, tambourine, bursts of bird-wing.
Camels raise eyebrows in elegant surprise,
exchange knowing glances
at the feats of the strong man, horses prancing.
The garden fills with noise and wonder,
disbelief miraculously suspended from a trapeze
      dangling
              without a net
above the heads of flowers
arranged in rows.

The camels forget to blink,
flowers forget to close their petals
as the sun sinks.

The circus plays out, cymbals scrape
and acrobats limp wearily to rest.
Big cats climb to stretch out on branches,
camels kneel and close their eyes
and dream of another life
beyond the garden walls.